Ladybird 🐞 Readers

What Color Is the Donkey?

Notes to teachers, parents, and carers

The *Ladybird Readers* Beginner level helps young language learners to become familiar with key conversational phrases in English. The language introduced has clear real-life applications, giving children the tools to hold their first conversations in English.

This book focuses on learning the principal colors in English, as well as introducing animal names.

There are some activities to do in this book. They will help children practice these skills:

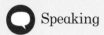 Speaking    Listening*   Reading

*To complete these activities, listen to the audio downloads available at **www.ladybirdeducation.co.uk**

Series Editor: Sorrel Pitts
Chants by Sorrel Pitts

LADYBIRD BOOKS

UK | USA | Canada | Ireland | Australia
India | New Zealand | South Africa

Ladybird Books is part of the Penguin Random House group of companies
whose addresses can be found at global.penguinrandomhouse.com.
www.penguin.co.uk   www.puffin.co.uk   www.ladybird.co.uk

Penguin
Random House
UK

Text inspired by *The Artist Who Painted a Blue Horse* by Eric Carle, first published in Great Britain by Puffin, 2011
This version first published by Ladybird Books 2024
001

Text and illustrations copyright © Penguin Random House LLC, 2011
Adapted text and artwork copyright © 2024 by Penguin Random House LLC
The moral right of the original author/illustrator has been asserted

ERIC CARLE'S name and signature logotype and the World of Eric Carle logo are trademarks of Penguin Random House LLC.
This edition published by arrangement with World of Eric Carle, an imprint of Penguin Young Readers Group, a division of Penguin Random House LLC.
All rights reserved including the right of reproduction in whole or in part in any form.
To find out more about Eric Carle and his books, please visit eric-carle.com. To learn about The Eric Carle Museum of Picture Book Art, please visit carlemuseum.org.

Printed in China

The authorized representative in the EEA is Penguin Random House Ireland, Morrison Chambers, 32 Nassau Street, Dublin D02 YH68

A CIP catalogue record for this book is available from the British Library

ISBN: 978-0-241-58781-2

All correspondence to:
Ladybird Books
Penguin Random House Children's
One Embassy Gardens, 8 Viaduct Gardens, London SW11 7BW

MIX
Paper | Supporting
responsible forestry
FSC® C018179

What Color Is the Donkey?

Inspired by
The Artist Who Painted a Blue Horse
by Eric Carle

What color is the horse?
It is blue!

What color is the crocodile?
It is red!

What color is the cow?
It is yellow!

What color is the rabbit?
It is pink!

What color is the lion?
It is green!

What color is the elephant?
It is orange!

What color is the fox?
It is purple!

What color is the polar bear?
It is black!

What color is the donkey?
It is blue, red, yellow,
pink, green,
orange, purple,
and black!

1 **Listen. Color in the words.**

1

| elephant | orange |

2

| purple | pink |

3

| polar bear | fox |

4

| yellow | green |

2 Listen. Put a  by the correct words. 🎧 📖

1 a The cow is yellow. ✓

b The horse is blue. ☐

2 a The fox is purple. ☐

b The rabbit is pink. ☐

3 a The lion is green. ☐

b The elephant is orange. ☐

4 a The rabbit is pink. ☐

b The crocodile is red. ☐

3 Read and clap!

What color is the horse?
The horse is blue. It is blue!

What color is the cow?
The cow is yellow. It is yellow!

What color is the lion?
The lion is green. It is green!

What color is the elephant?
The elephant is orange. It is orange!

What color do you like, like, like?
What color do you like?